PAUL CONRAD

Drawing the Line

* * * *

The Collected Works
of
America's Premier Political Cartoonist

"I AM NOT A CROOK." "I DON'T RECALL ANY IRAN-CONTRA CONNECTION." "I WAS NOT IN THE LOOP." "I DID NOT HAVE SEX WITH THAT WOMAN."

BY PAUL CONRAD

EDITED BY LES GUTHMAN

Los Angeles Times, a Times Mirror Company, Los Angeles, California

Acknowledgments

I must acknowledge the enormous help of my wife, Kay, in pulling together parts of this book. As my steadfast partner for more than 45 years, she's a first-class researcher, and her memory is better than mine. What's more, she has enriched my life beyond calculation. She discounts it, but I feel it's fair to say I wouldn't have become the cartoonist I am without her.

Also, I'm indebted to Les Guthman, who edited this volume, plowed through thousands of originals and prints, and helped make these choices and organize the book. He has been a friend since I met him as a young man, the son of my valued friend and *L.A. Times* colleague Edwin Guthman. The skills and help of Les, an outstanding journalist in his own right, have been monumental.

Paul Conrad, 1999

Book Development Manager: Carla Lazzareschi

Design: Tom Trapnell

Los Angeles Times

© 1999 Los Angeles Times

Published by the Los Angeles Times
Times Mirror Square, Los Angeles, California 90053
A Times Mirror Company

First printing April 1999

Printed in the U.S.A.

ISBN 1-883792-54-1

CONTENTS

R. GENN.

Paul Conrad: Prophet With a Pen

BY DOUG MARLETTE

Paul Conrad is more than a three-time Pulitzer Prize-winning cartoonist for the *Los Angeles Times*, more than a legend in cartooning and an institution in American journalism. He is a force of nature. The impact of Conrad cartoons can't be measured with Pulitzers or syndication figures, or even the hate mail they generate. You measure Conrad on the Richter scale.

Iowa-born and bred, Paul Conrad is as American and Midwestern as a Grant Wood painting, and his work reflects a fierce populism that is his birthright. For more than four decades he has comforted the afflicted and afflicted the comfortable. He has chronicled the last half of this demented and deranged century, throughout it all keeping a fixed point—like the North Star—by which we could set our moral bearings.

Conrad's 20/20 insight stands him squarely in the tradition of the Old Testament prophets. If Jeremiah had drawn, he would have drawn like Conrad. Paul Conrad is Isaiah with a Winsor and Newton brush. Amos with a Speedball pen. He is the prophet Nahum deploring the bloody city. Full of lies and booty—no end to the plunder! Hosts of slain, heaps of corpses, dead bodies without end.

Every line Conrad draws cries out like Nahum to the powers and principalities of 20th-century America: I will lift your skirts over your head and show your ass to the world.

Amen.

But prophets have never fit neatly into their surroundings, and Conrad is no exception. He was too much for the *Los Angeles Times* editorial page during Watergate, and they moved him onto the op-ed page. Why? Because Conrad doesn't draw, he erupts. He overwhelms the masthead and the finely tuned and delicately calibrated opinions of the good gray *Times* editorial page. They moved him to the op-ed page so everyone could breathe easier. The op-ed page, as Jules Feiffer once described it, is the free press apology for the First Amendment.

My test for greatness in cartoonists is simple. Do their images stick like Velcro in your brain? Do they tattoo themselves onto your soul? Who can ever forget Conrad's Nixon, nestled among reams and reams of Enemies Lists with the caption, "His Own Worst Enemy"?

Who can forget the expensive piece of dinnerware as it caught the image of a homeless woman rummaging through the garbage, and the caption, "Reflections on Mrs. Reagan's New White House China"?

I grew up in a South under siege by the civil rights movement and a country ravaged by the war in Vietnam. The opinions that flowed from the local editorial pages and their cartoonists could just as easily have been heard in the local barbershops, pool halls, truck stops and barbecue joints.

As a teenager I hungered for Conrad cartoons. I clipped and saved his drawings wherever I found them, savoring them like vintage wines. LBJ hypnotizes a photo of Ho Chi Minh, saying, "You are getting war-weary ... very war-weary," as his heavy-lidded staffers yawn and nap in the background.

A right-wing hardhat beats up an antiwar protester. "Son!" exclaims the assailant. "Dad!" the youngster replies. These cartoons were like oxygen to my brain.

As an aspiring cartoonist, I studied and learned from all the greats—Herblock, Mauldin, Wright, Oliphant—but there was something special about Conrad. I tried to imitate his style but failed miserably. I thank God. There are plenty of clones and faded carbons in this business. Oliphant clones, McNelly clones, but few Conrad clones.

The reason is simple. Conrad is inimitable. After all, how do you imitate nuclear fusion? It took me years to learn that Conrad was distinguished not by his line, though it was distinctive; not by his bite, though it too was sure; nor by his style and humor, though they were unique and gut-busting. What set Conrad apart was his heart.

In the objective, emotionally distant and often cold-blooded world of journalism, where values and passion are scorned, Conrad is our designated feeler. We live in an age when real feeling is discouraged, real passion is suspect and control is everything. We talk a lot about our feelings, but we don't actually let them get to us. We have become a nation of talk-show guests. And all of our talk about feelings is yet another subtle way of not feeling. It's all just an image.

We are Stepford citizens. That's why we need our Conrads now more than ever. He shows us how to be human.

The first time I met Paul Conrad, he and his wife, Kay, were entertaining a gaggle of us rapidly aging young snots at their house for drinks before dinner. As we stared at Conrad's Pulitzer Prizes on the wall and the *Time* magazine covers he had drawn, our host returned with our beverages, interrupting our oohs and aahs with his booming circus-ringmaster voice: "Yeah," he said, agreeing with our assessment, "Isn't that great?" No false modesty. No "Aw, shucks." Simple, uninhibited delight in what he had wrought.

I remember telling a colleague afterwards, "That is the key to Conrad's genius, and that is the key to greatness—authentic, unapologetic delight in oneself and one's art." Conrad was showing us

the secret of Picasso and Matisse, of Rilke and Joyce, of Dickens and Twain, the secret of every great artist—to be filled with awe and delight and wonder at the thoughts and images that flow from the darkest recesses and deepest cellars of your own soul.

Conrad may be the last of a breed. There arose in the 1980s, the Reagan Era, the kind of Teflon political cartoon—the kind that doesn't stick—that has no point of view. These drawings are widely reprinted, serviceable, mildly amusing—but they don't lay a finger on you!

Something's wrong when cartoonists take a keener interest in tracking their reprints in newsmagazines, syndication lists and Pulitzer Prize tallies than they do in the life-and-death issues they draw about every day.

Conrad is to these artists what the Great White Whale is to a school of guppies. They swim in the shallows; he plumbs the depths. Every day his ideas rise up like Moby Dick, and then he dives again. His readers, editors and colleagues are left standing dumbstruck, like the crew of the *Pequod*, scanning the horizon in uneasy silence, searching below, eyes darting left and right, harpoons at the ready, while gulls circle overhead until the mighty Conrad bursts forth again.

There is a tendency in this business for talent to burn out. But not Conrad. Never Conrad. He is on fire, and you can't put him out. He is the eternal flame. He spontaneously combusts every day, and, like the pillar of fire that led the children of Israel to the promised land by night, he illuminates the darkness and lights the way for us all.

Doug Marlette is the Pulitzer Prize-winning editorial cartoonist for Newsday. *He delivered this tribute in 1993.*

Conrad on Conrad

re all cartoonists liberal?

I'm sorry to say this, but I don't think a conservative has a sense of humor. I think you've got to have some kind of a sense of humor, no matter how serious it is. Nothing is funny to conservatives. They're all very serious: You know, the fate of the world, or the second coming of Christ, or the love of Allah depends on it.

There are some cartoonists who have tried very hard to be conservative. In fact, Bill Thomas, when he was editor of the *Los Angeles Times*, said to me, "Con, we're going to try something. I'm going to try and hire a conservative cartoonist."

I said, "Good luck. There is no such animal. That's an oxymoron."

In about three weeks, he came in and said, "Con, you're goddamn right. There's not a one of them I would hire. Because they're illustrators."

Now, illustrating in an editorial cartoon means to me that the person really doesn't know, doesn't have the background to say what he is saying. He or she only illustrates, but doesn't take a position ... doesn't say, "This is a crock," or "This is right on." You have to take a position. That's what the whole thing is about.

There was a six-paneled cartoon in the *Los Angeles Times* recently. I have no idea what it was about, but I did start counting the words. There were 235. Can you imagine that? I mean, why doesn't the man get into editorial writing? The thing was only 14 words shorter than Lincoln's Gettysburg Address. And I know what Lincoln was talking about!

Whenever I speak, I am always asked about becoming a cartoonist, how (or why) I started, and how to become a cartoonist.

That's like asking my dog how he became a golden retriever. Maybe I was born that way. I just

know, once I drew my first cartoon—for the *Daily Iowan* when I was a college art major at the University of Iowa—I've wanted to draw one every day since then.

Editorial cartoonists are a combination of editorialist, analyst and satirist.

And most of all, reader. And finally, an artist drawing an editorial opinion. But not an illustration.

It all began for me in the boys' restroom at St. Augustine's elementary school in Des Moines, Iowa. It was the habit of some of the older boys at St. Augustine's to indulge in a practice that I later found out was called graffiti.

They often wrote editorial comments about the St. Augustine school establishment on the restroom walls. My parents taught me that this was not a nice thing to do, and to this day I have never written an editorial comment on a restroom wall.

But one time, when I was eight or eight and a half, I did illustrate someone else's editorial comment on a restroom wall. As a result of that one cartoon, I learned several things: First, I learned that one picture is worth a thousand words, and that when the establishment gets mad, they always go after the cartoonist, not the editorial writers!

Second, I learned that it takes a big man to laugh at himself and that, tragically, many of the members of the establishment are not very big men.

Third, I learned that I could draw cartoons better than any other kid at St. Augustine's, and that people got excited about my drawings.

Last, I learned there was deep inside me an urge to say what I thought about life and the establishment to any and all who would look at my drawings.

There's too much to be concerned about, and I am a concerned citizen. Think of it—the hypocrisy of too many of our politicians. The irrelevance of much of our educational curriculum. And most of all, our failure to see that it is later than we think.

Since I began drawing 40 years ago, the problems facing our society have become progressively worse. All over the world, not just in the U.S.—Rwanda, Zaire, Botswana and, of course, Ireland, Bosnia and Israel. Much of it is destroying the humanity of man. The dignity of man.

I wish I had an easy answer. I don't. My function is to illustrate the problems and express concern. As far as I can see, the measure of man is his concern for the dignity of man, and thus for his own dignity.

I never stop being amazed by the fact that no matter how wild or fantastic a cartoon I draw might seem at the time, it's always eventually overtaken by events that prove to be even more wild or fantastic than I could ever imagine. In 1980, I thought it would be funny to draw Reagan's former movie costar, Bonzo the chimp, sleeping in the Lincoln bedroom—he was the kind of company to whom Reagan would offer that traditional honor in the White House, an honor previously reserved for a Churchill, or even a Frank Sinatra! But in the 1990s, Clinton took that beyond anything in my wildest imagination, turning it into a Motel 6 for fat-cat contributors and political hangers-on. Bring back Bonzo!

Where do my ideas come from? I wish I could answer that, but I can't. All I know is they happen. They seem to stem from the subconscious. Facts, figures, dates, deeds, all these feed the conscious mind. But no decent cartoon ever resulted from the conscious mind.

All the above ingredients, however, if left to the subconscious mind, seem to produce the final piece of satire the cartoonist has been seeking—the time element ranges from a split second to hours. You can't hurry the subconscious. But once it works, all you have to do is "draw the line." This may sound simplistic, and it probably is, but no one has ever explained to me how the synapses of the brain work. But work they do, if the information given the conscious is complete and correct.

However, there are times when blank follows blank. Nothing is working out. The synapses have days like that, too. So do quarterbacks. Fifteen seconds to go. The ball on the 50-yard line. His team behind by six. He goes to what is called the "Hail Mary" pass. It is caught by his wide receiver in the end zone—the extra point is added. Victory! Mary has done it again!

This, many times, has happened to me. Fifty minutes to go. No idea. And even if I had one, I still have to draw it. When this occurs, I simply put my head down and say a "Hail Mary." Call it a mantra, if you will, but it never fails.

And pretty soon here the idea is, all I have to do is draw it. If I could tell you how an idea happens—no one can—but they're a collection of everything you've read, all you've heard and seen. And somehow, if you can fit it together, an editorial cartoon happens.

I see the news on TV, hear it on the radio in the morning and read it in the newspapers. One thing follows another, to another, to another.

The ideas never just go, Pop, here it is, draw it. You have to develop them. Develop the idea, simplify it. Get the drawing as simple as you can, with few, if any, words in it. Then get into the line.

The cartoons are not done as works of art; they're opinions, and all I do is draw them. I draw what comes into my head after having reasoned the subject as thoroughly as I possibly can.

No amount of drawing saves a bad idea. I don't care what the drawing's like; if it's a good idea, it's marvelous. And I think that's the problem. We see just too few good ideas. This requires a lot of reading. Reading everything: opinions, both sides, all sides. And making up your mind who's right and who's wrong, and then going from there.

That's what I'm trying to do with these cartoons.

Humanitarian statements. I don't know how else to put it. I think they all have compassion, particularly for the guys who just don't have a prayer.

—Paul Conrad, 1999

"I Come to Bury Clinton, Not to Censure Him … "

"I COME TO BURY CLINTON, NOT TO CENSURE HIM …"

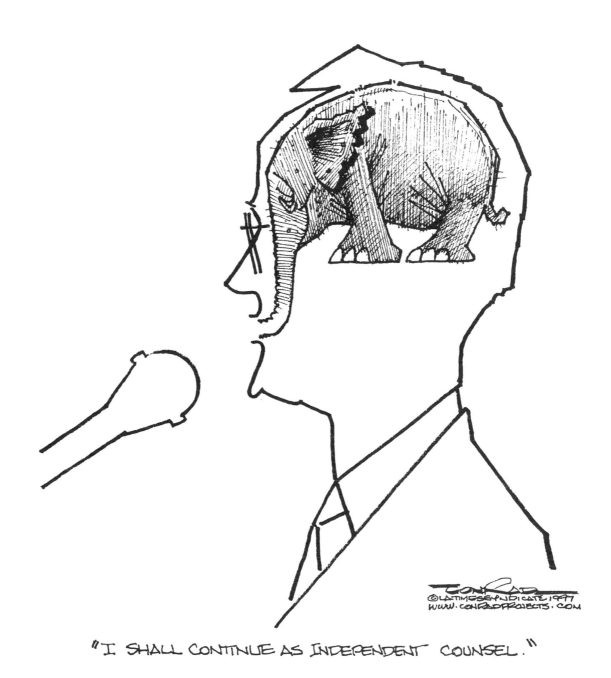

"I SHALL CONTINUE AS INDEPENDENT COUNSEL."

HIS OWN WORST ENEMY

THE FOUR BRANCHES OF GOVERNMENT

ORAL SAX

"BILL, AS LONG AS WE'RE NEUTERING BUDDY..."

"CONFESS!"

THE EVOLUTION OF INDEPENDENT COUNSEL KENNETH STARR

Linda Tripp Anxiously Awaits
Grand Jury Appearance

June 30, 1998

"IT'S A SUBPOENA FROM THE SPECIAL PROSECUTOR."

"IS SEX A HIGH CRIME, A MISDEMEANOR, OR WHAT?"

ANOTHER HATE CRIME

"THAT'S HIM! I'D RECOGNIZE THOSE DISTINGUISHING CHARACTERISTICS ANYWHERE!"

"SO, IMPEACH US..."

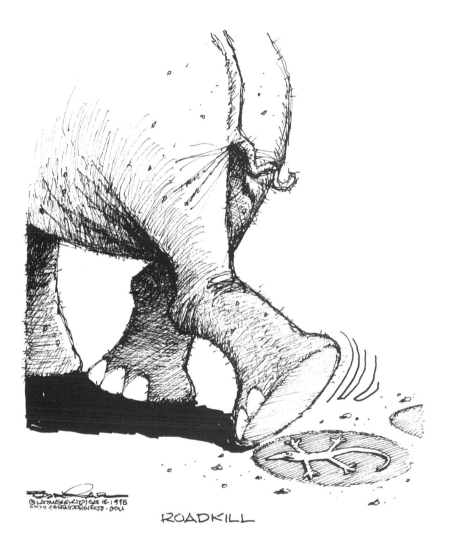

ROADKILL

"WHAT'D'YA MEAN WE FORGOT THE ROPE?"

DR. JEKYL AND MR. HYDE

THE CHRISTIAN RIGHT ARRIVING IN BETHLEHEM BEARING GIFTS
OF PARTISANSHIP, HYPOCRISY AND IMPEACHMENT.

"NOT THIS YEAR!"

HELEN OF TROY: THE FACE THAT LAUNCHED A THOUSAND SHIPS.

MONICA LEWINSKY: THE FACE THAT SUNK A THOUSAND HOPES.

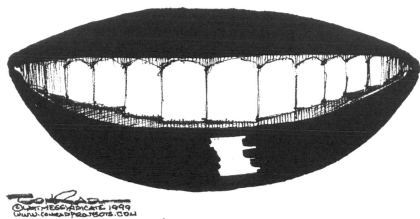

WHO WOULDN'T BELIEVE THOSE LIPS,
WHO WOULDN'T BELIEVE THOSE LIES...

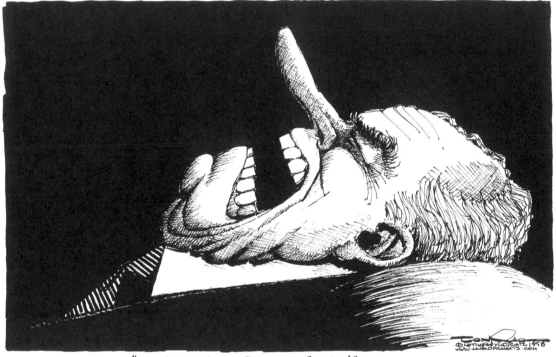

"IMPEACH THE BASTARD!"

"THIS IS ONLY A TEST!"

CONGRESSIONAL BIPARTISANSHIP

NOT ENOUGH VOTES TO DISMISS AND NOT ENOUGH VOTES TO CONVICT.

STATE OF THE UNION

STATE OF THE UNION

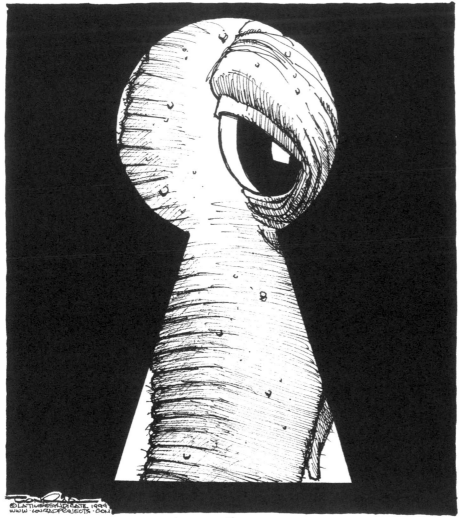

THE WITNESS

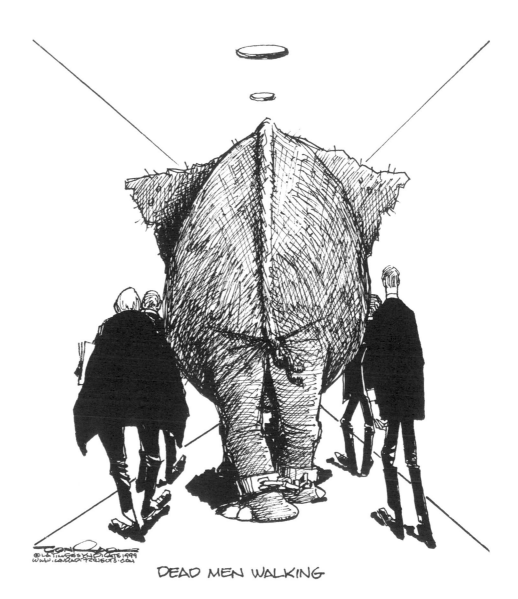

DEAD MEN WALKING

THE LEMMINGS

THE ROPE BROKE

"Say It Ain't So, Bill"

"SAY IT AINT SO, BILL!"

"HOW DOES MY PRIVATE SEX LIFE COMPARE TO THESE TWO WHO HAVE BEEN DOING THE SAME THING TO THE PEOPLE OF THIS COUNTRY FOR YEARS?"

ORDER LIFTING
BAN ON
GAYS

SENATOR JESSE HELMS THREATENS THE LIFE OF PRESIDENT BILL CLINTON

THE REAGAN~BUSH

Clinton Warns of Diminished Future
If Spending Cuts, Taxes Aren't Passed

February 18, 1993

CONGRESSIC PARK

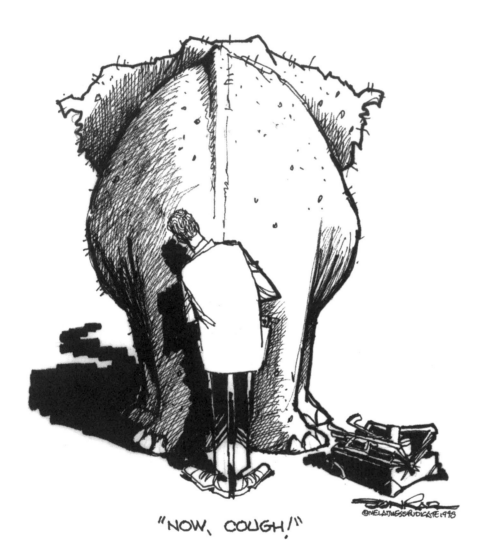

"NOW, COUGH!"

The Times Poll: By 2-1 Margin
Public Backs Health Care Plan

September 30, 1993

THE HEALTH CARE LESSON OF DR. DOLE

"BUT, OL WHITEWATER, IT JUST KEEPS ROLLING ALONG!"

"BUT IF I TAKE THE RAP, HILLARY, WHO'D BE PRESIDENT?"

Whitewater Panel Focuses
Microscope on First Lady

December 18, 1995

"GET CLINTON."

THE POLITICAL ASSASSIN

**Falwell Selling Tape
That Attacks Clinton**
Accusations include one
that alleges complicity by the
president in "countless murders."

May 14, 1994

"I AM NOT NOW NOR EVER HAVE I BEEN A
MEMBER OF THE CHRISTIAN COALITION."

CHECKED INFLATION.   TAMED THE DEFICIT.   FACED DOWN THE NRA

REDUCED UNEMPLOYMENT.   HAITI AND KUWAIT.   MIDEAST PEACE.

NOTHING FAILS LIKE SUCCESS

"WHY CAN'T WE ALL JUST GET ALONG?"—RODNEY KING

**Clinton Urges Americans
To Seek Common Ground**
President says nation needs
a "chorus of harmony."

July 7, 1995

YOUNG MAN WITH A HORN

"WON'T YOU COME HOME, BILL CLINTON, WON'T YOU COME HOME...?"

Tacking to the Right, Clinton
Borrows GOP Core Issues

July 17, 1995

"IT FOLLOWED ME HOME!"

"BUT, I DON'T INHALE!"

"SORRY ABOUT THAT." —MCNAMARA

A Confession That
Confirms Old Suspicions
Thirty years late, McNamara says, 'We
were wrong, terribly wrong, in Vietnam'

April 11, 1995

EISENHOWER

KENNEDY

CLIFFORD

ROSTOW

BUNDY

KISSINGER

JOHNSON

LAIRD

RUSK

NIXON

HAIG

WESTMORELAND

McNAMARA'S BAND

THOSE WHO OPPOSED A SPECIAL PROSECUTOR FOR WATERGATE, CONTRAGATE AND IRANGATE BECAUSE "NO LAW HAD BEEN BROKEN"...

...WHO NOW FAVOR A SPECIAL PROSECUTOR TO NAIL CLINTON.

"I AM THE GHOST OF CHRISTMAS PAST!"

"TALK RADIO"

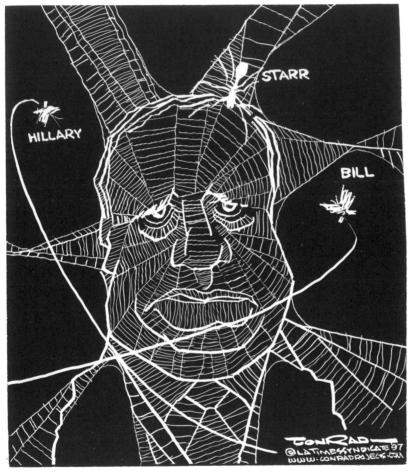

WEB

CLINTON IS THINKING ABOUT PRESIDENTIAL PARDONS.

AFTER ALL...

NIXON PARDONED JIMMY HOFFA..

FORD PARDONED NIXON...

...AND BUSH PARDONED ABRAMS, M°FARLANE, WEINBERGER, HAMMER, AND OTHERS.

"I'LL CALL OFF YOUR SPECIAL PROSECUTOR IF YOU'LL CALL OFF MINE."

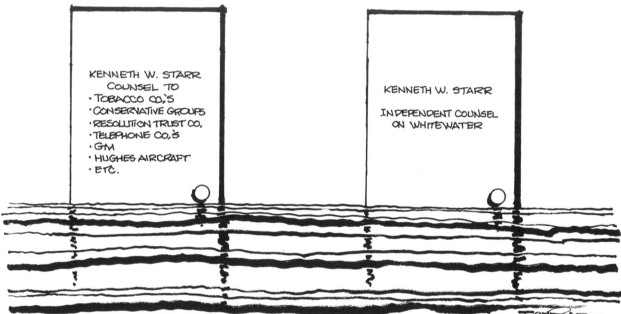

"Eye of Newt"

EYE OF NEWT, TOE OF HELMS,
WOOL OF DORNAN, TONGUE OF DOLE,
— SHAKESPEARE

NEWT

Gingrich Speech Debuts
His Kinder, Gentler Side

January 5, 1995

"FRIAR NEWT, I HEREBY DUB THEE 'SON OF REAGAN HOOD' WHO
ROBS FROM THE POOR AND GIVES TO THE RICH!"

NEWTPOLEON I

Taking the Hill, Emboldened
By Their Sweep Into Office,
Congressional Republicans
Are Full of Revolution

January 8, 1995

NEWT IS A FOUR LETTER WORD

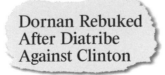

Dornan Rebuked
After Diatribe
Against Clinton

January 26, 1995

Armey Remark
About Democrat
Sparks Furor

January 28, 1995

BALANCED BUDGET AMENDMENT

House Balanced Budget
Amendment Approved

January 17, 1995

GOPAC, SON OF CREEP (NIXON'S COMMITTEE TO REELECT THE PRESIDENT)

Funding of Gingrich
PAC Raises Questions

January 29, 1995

Orphan Annie

Gingrich Blasts Critics of
GOP Social Service Cuts

March 8, 1995

WOE TO THE LEGISLATURES OF INFAMOUS LAWS.... WHO REFUSE JUSTICE TO THE UNFORTUNATE AND CHEAT THE POOR AMONG MY PEOPLE OF THEIR RIGHTS, WHO MAKE WIDOWS THEIR PREY AND ROB THE ORPHAN. —ISAIAH 10: 1-2

MIND OVER MATTER

The Bill of Rights

i *provided in the* FIRST TEN AMENDMENTS TO THE CONSTITUTION OF THE UNITED STATES
Effective December 15, 1791

Preamble

The conventions of a number of the States having at the time of their adopting the Constitution, expressed a desire, in order to prevent misconstruction or abuse of its powers, that further declaratory and restrictive clauses should be added: And as extending the ground of public confidence in the Government, will best insure the beneficient ends of its institution.

1   **Right** *to Freedom of Religion, Speech, Press, Assembly, Petition.*

2   **Right** *to Keep and Bear Arms.*

3   **Rights** *on Quartering of Soldiers.*

4   **Right** *against Unreasonable Search and Seizure.*

5   **Right** *to Protection of Persons and Property.*

6   **Rights** *of Persons Accused of Crime.*

7   **Right** *of Trial by Jury.*

8   **Right** *to Protection Against Excessive Fines, Bail, Punishment.*

9   **Rights** *not enumerated retained by the people.*

10   **Rights** *reserved to the States and the People.*
      The powers not delegated to the United States by the Constitution, nor prohibited by it to the States, are reserved to the States respectively, or to the people.

REPUBLICANS' CONTRACT ON AMERICA

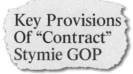

Key Provisions
Of "Contract"
Stymie GOP

March 10, 1995

ANOTHER UNWED MOTHER ON AFDC WHO AFTER TWO YEARS WILL BE CUT OFF TO GO FIND A JOB.

GOP Budget Plans Would
Put Burden on the Poor
Republicans agree the needy
will be the hardest hit

October 29, 1995

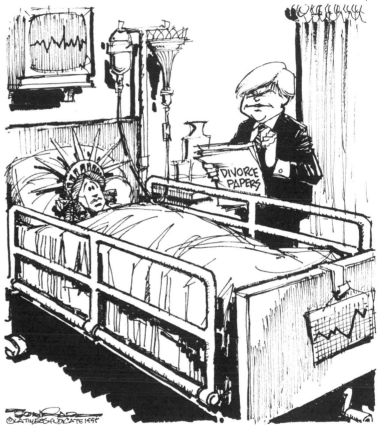

"YOU'RE NOT YOUNG ENOUGH OR PRETTY ENOUGH TO BE THE WIFE OF THE PRESIDENT. AND BESIDES, YOU HAVE CANCER."

"THAT'S A CONTRACT, NOT A WARRANTY!"

"I AM NOT A CROOK!"

Documents Raise Questions
On Gingrich's House Ethics

March 20, 1995

SNOW WHITE AND THE SEVEN DWARFS

Gingrich Makes Splash
Testing Waters

June 11, 1995

RESERVED FOR SENATOR PACKWOOD

WE ALREADY HAVE A THIRD PARTY

Clinton Assails GOP for Backing
Bills Linked to Special Interests

August 2, 1995

WHAT ETHICS COMMITTEE ?

Major GOPAC Donors Got
Special Access, Files Show

December 17, 1995

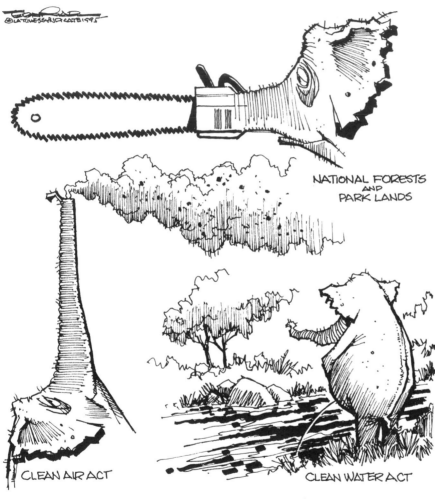

NATIONAL FORESTS
AND
PARK LANDS

CLEAN AIR ACT

CLEAN WATER ACT

THE ENVIRONMENTALISTS

It's "Big Sugar"
vs. "Big Swamp"
In Everglades Vote
A close and bitterly
contested campaign ...

October 18, 1996

THE C.E.O. WHO SCREWED-UP.   THE PART-TIME EMPLOYEE WHO SCREWED-UP.

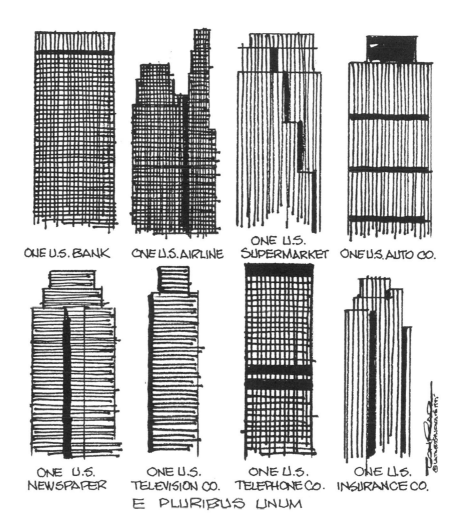

ONE U.S. BANK   ONE U.S. AIRLINE   ONE U.S. SUPERMARKET   ONE U.S. AUTO CO.

ONE U.S. NEWSPAPER   ONE U.S. TELEVISION CO.   ONE U.S. TELEPHONE CO.   ONE U.S. INSURANCE CO.

E PLURIBUS UNUM

93

THERE IS A YOUNG LADY WHO LIVES IN A SHOE,
THE COMPANY MAKES MILLIONS, SHE ONLY MAKES TWO.

WHERE THE FASHION MOGULS GO TO SHOP.

EVOLUTION OF AN ELEPHANT INTO A NEWT

Unyielding GOP Freshmen
Lead Balanced Budget Siege

December 11, 1995

THANKSGIVING TURKEY

Can Gingrich Hold His
Tongue for Good of Party?

December 14, 1995

FOSSILIZED EMBRYO OF A NEWT GINGRICH DINOSAUR

"HAS HILLARY RECANTED YET?"

Papers Bolster Link Between
First Lady, Travel Scandal

January 11, 1996

"THE INQUISITION WILL CONTINUE UNTIL NOVEMBER FIFTH."

Republicans Allege Stalling
On Whitewater Documents

February 23, 1996

MY LAI COVERUP.

ILLEGAL WAR AGAINST
NICARAGUA + EL SALVADOR.

IRAN-CONTRA COVERUP.

'TURKEY SHOOT' IN IRAQ.

PANAMA + GRENADA.

POWELL

MY AMERICAN JOURNEY

Powell Weighs Risks
Of the Political Battlefield
Retired general mulls
presidential run

September 17, 1995

THE BOB AND ELIZABETH SHOW

"WHAT BOB REALLY MEANS...."

"GIVE ME FAITH, HOPE AND HILLARY!"

"WHITEWATERGATE"

'GET EVEN' TIME

THE FARCE IS BACK

**Gingrich Survives New Try
To Unseat Him as Speaker**
Even some key GOP lieutenants
may have participated.

July 17, 1997

"I Was Out of the Loop"

"I WAS OUT OF THE LOOP."

NO HEART   NO BRAINS   NO COURAGE

"TO JIMMY CARTER... IT'S ALL HIS FAULT!"

THE REAGAN BUSH

PROSPECTIVE JURORS FOR THE NORTH TRIAL WHO HAVE NO
KNOWLEDGE OF THE IRAN-CONTRA AFFAIR.

PARDONS HAPPEN

Bush Pardons Weinberger,
5 Others in Iran-Contra

December 25, 1992

"WHAT'S GOOD ENOUGH FOR ME FOR DRUNK DRIVING OUGHT TO BE GOOD ENOUGH FOR CASPER WEINBERGER FOR LYING TO CONGRESS."

JUSTICE THURGOOD MARSHALL SAT HERE

CNN'S PETER ARNETT
REPORTING FROM BAGHDAD.

U.S. MEDIA REPORTING
FROM PENTAGON BRIEFING.

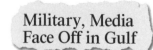

Military, Media
Face Off in Gulf

January 12, 1991

REAGANSTEIN'S SADDAM

WHAT TO DO ABOUT IRAQGATE

"DEAD AT LAST! DEAD AT LAST! THANK GOD ALMIGHTY, THEY'RE DEAD AT LAST!"

1963 — 1996

"WHAT DO YOU WANTA' BE IF YOU GROW UP?"

GEORGE BUSH'S RUNNING MATES

"WHEN IS CLINTON GONNA' TELL US THE TRUTH ABOUT HIS DRAFT THING?"

"I WAS OUT OF THE LOOPS."

"FOUR MORE WEEKS! FOUR MORE WEEKS!"

PILLORY CLINTON

Hillary-Bashing Becoming
Part of GOP Campaign

August 19, 1992

RESULTS OF HURRICANE REAGAN-BUSH. DAMAGE ESTIMATE: $4 TRILLION

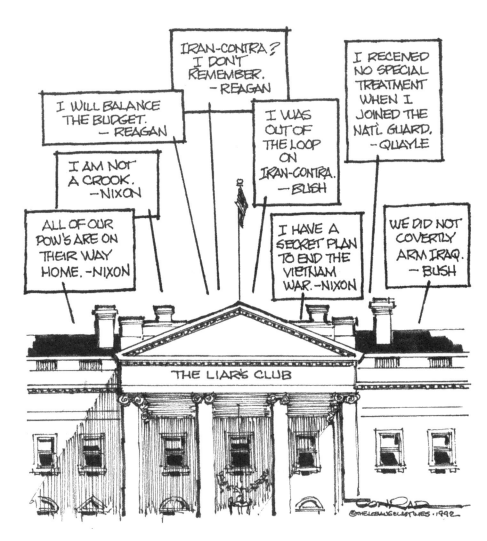

"Where Did We Go Wrong?"

"WHERE DID WE GO WRONG?"

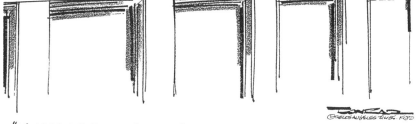

"YOU LOOK FOR A CERTAIN COMPATIBILITY. A BROAD COMPATIBILITY. WITH YOUR OWN PHILOSOPHY IN LOOKING FOR JUDGES." —REAGAN

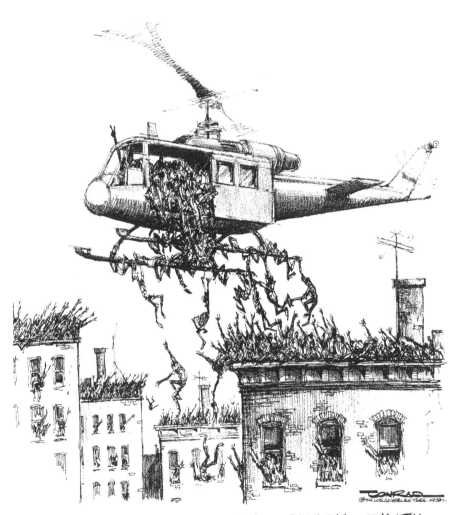

U.S. DECLARES VICTORY IN WAR ON POVERTY AND PULLS OUT. — NEWS ITEM

REFLECTIONS ON MRS. REAGAN'S NEW WHITE HOUSE CHINA

THE SORCERER'S APPRENTICE

White House Clarifies
Role of Astrology

May 10, 1988

"A POISONED APPLE. THE SLEEPING DEATH FOR THE ENVIRONMENTAL PROTECTION AGENCY! PERFECT!"

"YOU'RE ON YOUR OWN, KID, ONCE YOU'RE BORN!"

"MY CANDLE BURNS AT BOTH ENDS; IT WILL NOT LAST THE NIGHT; BUT, AH, MY FOES, AND, OH, MY FRIENDS —IT GIVES A PRETTY LIGHT."
— EDNA ST. VINCENT MILLAY

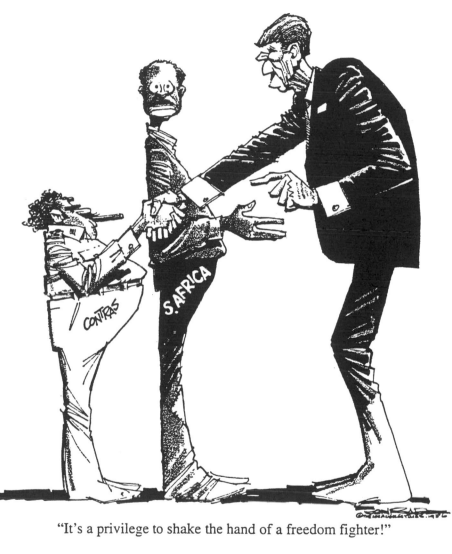

"It's a privilege to shake the hand of a freedom fighter!"

"HOW COME I WAS TO BLAME FOR THE 52 HOSTAGES WHO GOT OUT ALIVE AND NOBODY'S TO BLAME FOR THE 260 MARINES WHO DIED IN BEIRUT?"

... and to our children and to their children and to their childrens' children. I leave the remainder of my estate, the debt of two and one-half trillion dollars....

DRAWING UP THE WILL

"A Grin Without a Cat"

"HAVE YOU CHECKED MY RATING IN THE POLLS LATELY?"

CALIFORNIA SYNDROME

"NOW THAT THE ISSUES HAVE BECOME MORE MANAGEABLE..."

"WHERE DID WE GO WRONG?"

"His Own Worst Enemy"

His Own Worst Enemy

"He says he's from the phone company . . ."

"I'm sorry — I don't recognize any of them . . . !"

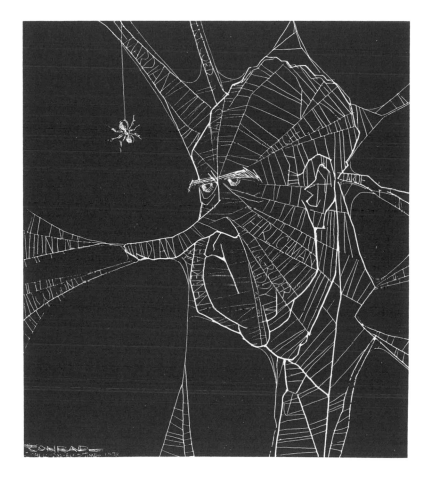

"HERR HALDEMAN, RUN IRS AUDITS ON ALL JEWS GIVING TO THE DEMOCRATS!"

O THAT I WERE AS GREAT AS MY GRIEF, OR LESSER THAN MY NAME!
OR THAT I COULD FORGET WHAT I HAVE BEEN!
OR NOT REMEMBER WHAT I MUST BE NOW!
KING RICHARD II. ACT III, SCENE III

"ALAS, POOR AGNEW, MITCHELL, STANS, EHRLICHMAN, HALDEMAN, DEAN, KALMBACH, LA RUE, MARDIAN, STRACHAN, M'CORD, LIDDY, CHAPIN, HUNT, COLSON, KROGH, MAGRUDER, YOUNG—I KNEW THEM..."

THE KING IS DEAD... LONG LIVE THE PRESIDENCY!

"I WAS NOT A DRUNK!"

COVER-UP OF THE COVER-UP

THE FINAL COVER-UP: NIXON LIBRARY GETTING LETTERS AND TAPES FROM NATIONAL ARCHIVES.

Where Have All the Leaders Gone?

"A Letter From the Front"

A LETTER FROM THE FRONT

"First, Premier Ky, you must learn the principles of democracy…"

'…the Great Buddha has answered our prayers!'

"Son...!"   "Dad...!"

"Stand back everybody! He's got a bomb!!"

There are cats and there are fat cats…

Robert Kennedy Shot …

June 5, 1968

"If you don't mind, Senator Kennedy, I'd rather walk…"

"Oh, it's just kind of a hobby with me…!"

"… one nation, divisible, with liberty and justice for some."

"It only hurts when I laugh!"

"Profiles in Courage"

PROFILES IN COURAGE

ONE MAN, TWENTY EIGHT MILLION VOTES.

"SAY GOODNIGHT, GRACIE!"

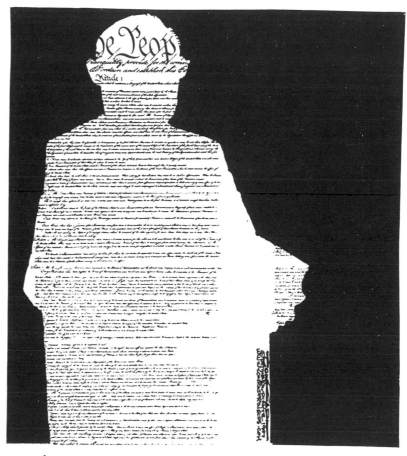

JUSTICE WILLIAM BRENNAN, 1906-1997

Side One

SGT. PEPPER'S LONELY HEARTS CLUB BAND
It was twenty years ago today,
Sgt. Pepper taught the band to play
They've been going in and out of style
But they're guaranteed to raise a smile.
So may I introduce to you
The act you've known for all these years,
Sgt. Pepper's Lonely Hearts Club Band.
We're Sgt. Pepper's Lonely Hearts Club
Band,
We hope you will enjoy the show,
We're Sgt. Pepper's Lonely Hearts Club
Band,
Sit back and let the evening go.
Sgt. Pepper's lonely, Sgt. Pepper's lonely,
Sgt. Pepper's Lonely Hearts Club Band.
It's wonderful to be here,
It's certainly a thrill.
You're such a lovely audience,
We'd like to take you home with us,
We'd love to take you home.
I don't really want to stop the show,
But I thought that you might like to
know,
That the singer's going to sing a song,
And he wants you all to sing along.
So let me introduce to you
The one and only Billy Shears
And Sgt. Pepper's Lonely Hearts Club
Band.

A LITTLE HELP FROM MY FRIENDS
A little help from my friends
What would you think if I sang out of
tune,
Would you stand up and walk out on me.
Lend me your ears and I'll sing you a
song,
And I'll try not to sing out of key.
I get by with a little help from my friends,
I get high with a little help from my
friends,
Going to try with a little help from my
friends.
What do I do when my love is away.
(Does it worry you to be alone)
How do I feel by the end of the day
(Are you sad because you're on your own)
No I get by with a little help from my
friends,
Do you need anybody,
I need somebody to love.
Could it be anybody
I want somebody to love.
Would you believe in a love at first sight,
Yes I'm certain that it happens all the
time.
What do you see when you turn out the
light,
I can't tell you, but I know it's mine.

That grow so incredibly high.
Newspaper taxis appear on the shore,
Waiting to take you away.
Climb in the back with your head in the
clouds,
And you're gone.
Lucy in the sky with diamonds,
Picture yourself on a train in a station,
With Plasticine porters with looking
glass ties,
Suddenly someone is there at the
turnstile,
The girl with the kaleidoscope eyes.

GETTING BETTER
It's getting better all the time
I used to get mad at my school
The teachers that taught me weren't cool
You're holding me down, turning me
round
Filling me up with your rules.
I've got to admit it's getting better
A little better all the time
I have to admit it's getting better
It's getting better since you've been mine.
Me used to be a angry young man
Me hiding me head in the sand
You gave me the word
I finally heard
I'm doing the best that I can.
I've got to admit it's getting better
I used to be cruel to my woman
I beat her and kept her apart from the
things that she loved
Man I was mean but I'm changing my
scene
And I'm doing the best that I can.
I admit it's getting better
A little better all the time
Yes I admit it's getting better
It's getting better since you've been mine.

FIXING A HOLE
I'm fixing a hole where the rain gets in
And stops my mind from wandering
Where it will go
I'm filling the cracks that ran through
the door
And kept my mind from wandering
Where it will go
And it really doesn't matter if I'm wrong
I'm right
Where I belong I'm right
Where I belong.
See the people standing there who
disagree and never win
And wonder why they don't get in my door.
I'm painting my room in a
colourful way
And when my mind is wandering
There I will go.

For so many years. Bye, bye
Father snores as his wife gets into her
dressing gown
Picks up the letter that's lying there
Standing alone at the top of the stairs
She breaks down and cries to her husband
Daddy our baby's gone.
Why would she treat us so thoughtlessly
How could she do this to me.
She (We never thought of ourselves)
is leaving (Never a thought for ourselves)
home (We struggled hard all
            our lives to get by)
She's leaving home after living alone
For so many years. Bye, Bye
Friday morning at nine o'clock she is far
away
Waiting to keep the appointment she
made
Meeting a man from the motor trade.
She   What did we do that was wrong
is having   We didn't know it was wrong
fun   Fun is the one thing that
            money can't buy
Something inside that was always denied
For so many years. Bye, Bye
She's leaving home bye bye

BEING FOR THE BENEFIT OF MR. KITE!
For the benefit of Mr. Kite
There will be a show tonight on
trampoline
The Hendersons will all be there
Late of Pablo Fanque's fair—what a scene
Over men and horses hoops and garters
Lastly through a hogshead of real fire!
In this way Mr. K. will challenge the
world!
The celebrated Mr. K.
Performs his feat on Saturday at
Bishopsgate
The Hendersons will dance and sing
As Mr. Kite flys through the ring don't
be late
Messrs. K. and H. assure the public
Their production will be second to none
And of course Henry The Horse dances
the waltz!
The band begins at ten to six
When Mr. K. performs his tricks without
a sound
And Mr. H. will demonstrate
Ten somersets he'll undertake on
solid ground
Having been some days in preparation
A splendid time is guaranteed for all
And tonight Mr. Kite is topping the bill.
John Lennon & Paul McCartney

SGT. PEPPERS LONELY HEARTS CLUB BAND

DOROTHY BUFFUM CHANDLER, 1901-1997

THE SHADOW AND THE IMAGE

THE BRITISH CROWN HAS LOST A PRIZE JEWEL

PIETA

WE COME TO PRAISE CESAR, NOT TO BURY HIM.

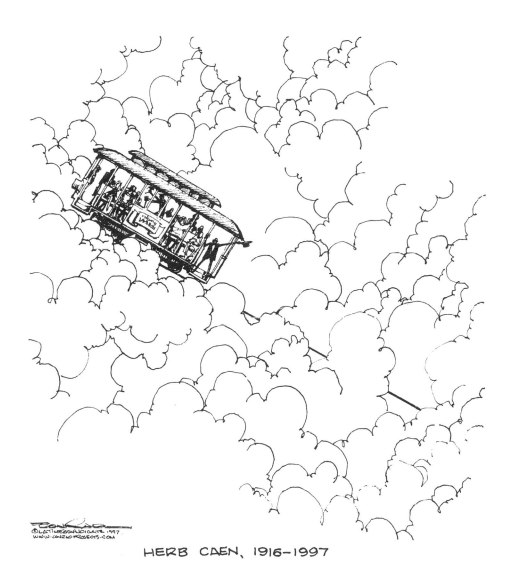

HERB CAEN, 1916-1997

THURGOOD MARSHALL 1908-1993

THE KING IS DEAD; LONG LIVE THE PEACE,